Terrific practice for White Rose Maths from CGP!

This brilliant CGP workbook is matched to the White Rose Maths Scheme of Learning — great for helping pupils work on their skills.

It's jam-packed with questions for every block and small step of the Year 6 Autumn Term — so you know it has everything pupils need.

Plus there are plenty of Problem Solving and Reasoning questions to check they know their stuff. Oh, and don't forget, we've included the answers to every question online — just scan the QR code at the end of the contents page. You're welcome!

What CGP is all about

Our sole aim here at CGP is to produce the highest quality books — carefully written, immaculately presented and dangerously close to being funny.

Then we work our socks off to get them out to you — at the cheapest possible prices.

Contents

Block 4 — Fractions B

Block 5 — Converting Units

Online Extras

The **answers** to every question in the book are available **online** — to find them, scan the QR code on the left or go to cgpbooks.co.uk/rose

Published by CGP

Editors:
Sammy El-Bahrawy, Shaun Harrogate, Alison Palin, Caley Simpson, Julie Wakeling

"White Rose Maths" is a registered trade mark of White Rose Education Ltd.
Please note that CGP is not associated with White Rose Maths or White Rose Education in any way.
This book does not include any official questions and is not endorsed by White Rose Education.

ISBN: 978 1 83774 182 3

With thanks to Emily Forsberg, Alison Griffin and Glenn Rogers for the proofreading.
With thanks to Jade Sim for the copyright research.

Clipart from Corel®

Printed by Elanders Ltd, Newcastle upon Tyne.
Based on the classic CGP style created by Richard Parsons.

About This Book

- This book matches the <u>White Rose Maths</u> Scheme of Learning for <u>Year 6 Autumn Term</u>.
- It's split up into <u>blocks</u>, with each <u>small step</u> covered on one or two pages.

There are questions on all the <u>key content</u>, giving great practice for every step.

We've included plenty of <u>pictorial</u> questions throughout.

Pupils might find it helpful to use <u>concrete objects</u> to answer some questions.

Pencils show pupils where to write their answers.

<u>Speech bubbles</u> may give prompts for <u>discussion</u> or <u>hints</u> for answering questions.

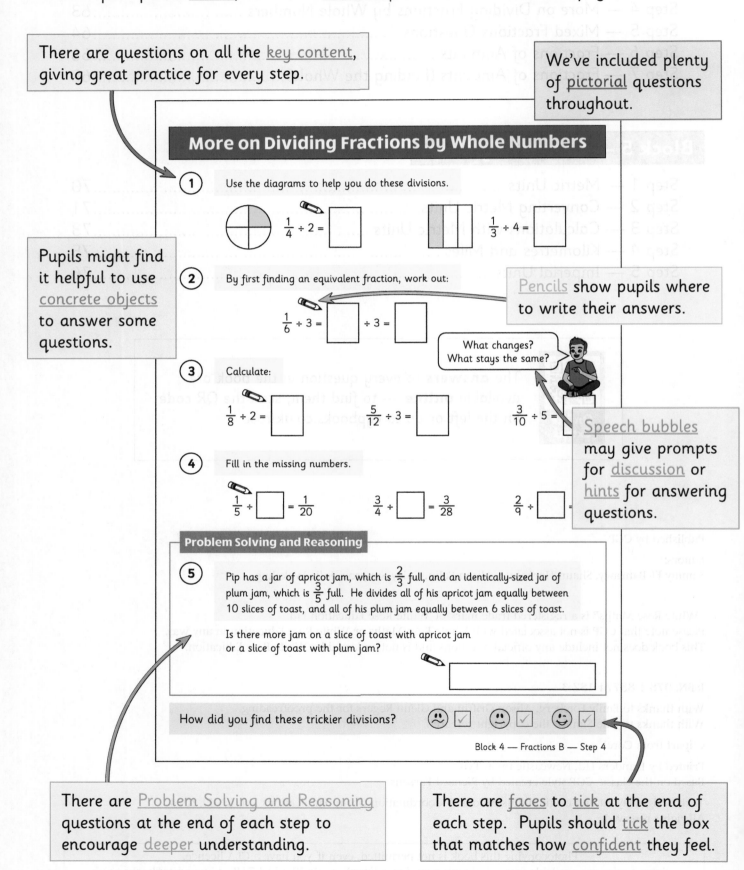

More on Dividing Fractions by Whole Numbers

1 Use the diagrams to help you do these divisions.

$\frac{1}{4} \div 2 =$ ⬜ $\frac{1}{3} \div 4 =$ ⬜

2 By first finding an equivalent fraction, work out:

$\frac{1}{6} \div 3 =$ ⬜ $\div 3 =$ ⬜

What changes? What stays the same?

3 Calculate:

$\frac{1}{8} \div 2 =$ ⬜ $\frac{5}{12} \div 3 =$ ⬜ $\frac{3}{10} \div 5 =$ ⬜

4 Fill in the missing numbers.

$\frac{1}{5} \div$ ⬜ $= \frac{1}{20}$ $\frac{3}{4} \div$ ⬜ $= \frac{3}{28}$ $\frac{2}{9} \div$ ⬜ $=$

Problem Solving and Reasoning

5 Pip has a jar of apricot jam, which is $\frac{2}{3}$ full, and an identically-sized jar of plum jam, which is $\frac{3}{5}$ full. He divides all of his apricot jam equally between 10 slices of toast, and all of his plum jam equally between 6 slices of toast.

Is there more jam on a slice of toast with apricot jam or a slice of toast with plum jam?

How did you find these trickier divisions? ☹ ☑ 🙂 ☑ 😀 ☑

Block 4 — Fractions B — Step 4

There are <u>Problem Solving and Reasoning</u> questions at the end of each step to encourage <u>deeper</u> understanding.

There are <u>faces</u> to <u>tick</u> at the end of each step. Pupils should <u>tick</u> the box that matches how <u>confident</u> they feel.

Numbers to 1 000 000

(1) What number is shown?

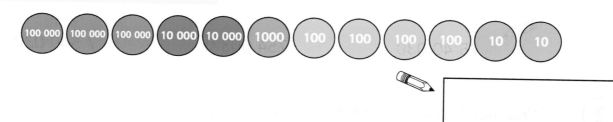

✏️ [ ]

(2) Fill in the digits in the place value columns to show each number.

✏️

Thousands			Ones		
H	T	O	H	T	O

758 249

804 960

60 017

(3) Write the missing numbers in these number sentences.

✏️ 408 571 = 400 000 + [ ] + [ ] + [ ] + 1

✏️ 900 000 + 70 000 + 400 + 50 + 8 = [ ]

Problem Solving and Reasoning

(4) Chantelle writes the number 247 563. She says:

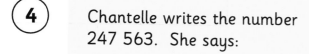

If I add 3000 to my number, the digits in two columns will change.

Do you agree with Chantelle? How do you know?

[ ]

How confident are you with big numbers? ☑ ☑ ☑

Numbers to 10 000 000

(1) Circle the correct way of writing this 7-digit number.

75 40 030   754 003 0   7 540 030

(2) What numbers are shown by the diagrams below?

Can you think of different ways to partition this number by changing the part-whole model?

| 2 000 000 | 823 000 | 164 |

M	HTh	TTh	Th	H	T	O

(3) Fill in the gaps in the number sentences.

= 6 000 000 + 700 000 + 5000 + 200 + 10 + 7

8 040 932 =   + 40 000 +   +   +

3

4 Draw lines to match each number to the correct value of the digit '3'.

4 503 227   688 321   3 457 800   9 032 648

300   3000   30 000   300 000   3 000 000

5 Start at 5 850 300 and count down two steps of 100 000.

5 850 300

6 Write the number that is 40 000 greater than the number shown below.

Millions	Thousands			Ones		
O	H	T	O	H	T	O
6	0	5	1	2	6	6

Problem Solving and Reasoning

7 A number is partitioned into two numbers, shown in the place value chart. Use the chart to work out the original number.

M	HTh	TTh	Th	H	T	O
●	● ●	● ● ● ● ●				
	● ● ● ● ● ●	● ● ● ● ●	● ● ● ● ● ●	○	● ●	● ● ● ● ● ● ● ● ●

How do you feel about these huge numbers? 🙁 ☑   🙂 ☑   😉 ☑

4

Reading and Writing Numbers to 10 000 000

1 Write the number shown on this bar model in words.

1 000 000	650 000

> Say the number out loud before you write it down.

2 Write the number seven million, two hundred and fifty thousand, four hundred and sixteen in numerals.

3 Write the number 5 308 611 in words.

4 Fill in the place value chart to show the number four million, eighteen thousand, five hundred and two. Then write it in numerals.

Millions	Thousands			Ones		
O	H	T	O	H	T	O

5 Write the amount each painting sold for in numerals.

"My painting, 'dog on a scooter', sold for two and a half million pounds!"

"My painting, 'dog on a treadmill', sold for ninety thousand pounds more."

£ _____

£ _____

6 Write in words the number that is 3 000 000 greater than the number shown.

100 000	200 000	300 000	400 000	500 000	600 000	700 000	800 000	900 000
10 000	20 000	30 000	40 000	50 000	60 000	70 000	80 000	90 000
1000	2000	3000	4000	5000	6000	7000	8000	9000
100	200	300	400	500	600	700	800	900
10	20	30	40	50	60	70	80	90
1	2	3	4	5	6	7	8	9

Problem Solving and Reasoning

7 Start with the number 9 247 683. Decrease every digit by 2.
Then swap the digits in the millions and tens places.
Then swap the digits in the ones and thousands places.
Write out the final number in words.

Can you swap between words and numerals?

Multiplying and Dividing by Powers of 10

1 Work out the following calculations.

3678 × 1000 = ☐

52 600 ÷ ☐ = 526

☐ ÷ 10 = 9106

1480 × ☐ = 1 480 000

2 Find the following amounts.

The number that is 1000 times the size of 702. ☐

One hundredth of 820 000. ☐

3 Circle the correct word(s) to complete each sentence.

32 is one   hundredth / thousandth of 32 000.

2600 is   ten / one hundred times the size of 260.

751 is one   tenth / hundredth of 75 100.

Can you do Q4 without working out the answers first?

4 Draw lines to match calculations with the same answers.

570 000 ÷ 10 ÷ 10   570 × 100 × 10   57 × 10 × 10 × 10

57 000 ÷ 10 × 100   5700 × 100 ÷ 10   570 000 ÷ 100

Problem Solving and Reasoning

5 Theo divides a number by 100, then multiplies his answer by 10.
He then divides by 1000 and multiplies by 10 again.

What single calculation could he have done instead? ☐

Can you wield the powers of ten?

Number Lines to 10 000 000

1 Write the number the arrow is pointing to.

2 Draw an arrow from each number to its position on the number line.

three and a half million 　　　　 5 750 000 　　　　 7 500 000

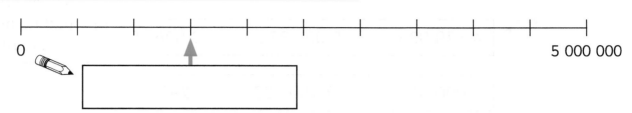

3 Circle the **blue** arrow that is pointing to the number 3 000 000 and the **red** arrow that is pointing to the number 6 500 000.

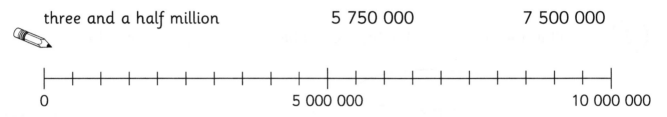

Problem Solving and Reasoning

4 Zahra and Joe each draw a number line and mark a number on it with an arrow.

Joe says, "My number is smaller because it is further to the left on the number line."

Is Joe correct? Explain your answer.

Zahra

Joe

Have you got your numbers in a line?

8

Comparing and Ordering Numbers

1 Circle the smallest number in each set.

| 4 579 036 | 5 002 372 | 3 996 599 |

| 2 090 465 | 2 150 302 | 290 879 |

| 6 540 027 | 6 495 720 | 6 540 072 |

> What should you look at first when putting numbers in order?

2 Fill in the correct symbol (<, > or =) between each pair of numbers.

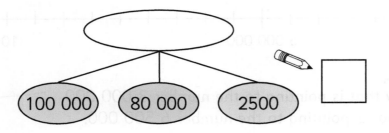

(100 000) (80 000) (2500) □

?
| 100 000 | 82 250 |

| M | HTh | TTh | Th | H | T | O |

□ four and a half million

2 000 000 + 925 000 + 300 + 14 □ 2 925 341

3 Write the numbers shown in this place value chart in ascending order.

| Millions | Thousands | | | Ones | | |
O	H	T	O	H	T	O
3	2	5	1	4	0	1
3	0	7	6	5	3	0
3	2	3	8	7	4	9

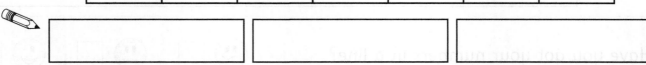

4 Draw arrows to connect the numbers in order, starting with the smallest.

769 830

7 007 586

770 524

7 100 985

7 068 264

5 Put the numbers in the box in descending order.

4 020 510   4 002 150   4 200 501   4 020 501

6 Put these intergalactic cities in order, starting with the largest population.

City	Population
Star City	6 240 362
New Tokyo	599 835
Comet Landing	6 204 975
Stow-on-the-Moon	642 894
Los Meteoritos	5 402 204

Problem Solving and Reasoning

7 By rearranging the digits in the box, how many different numbers can you make to go in the gap to make the statement correct?

2 485 962 < _____ < 2 490 260

| 2 | 4 | 8 | 6 | 0 | 9 | 1 |

Can you get your numbers in order?

Rounding Whole Numbers

1 Draw an arrow to show the position of 4 750 000 on the number line. Then use the number line to round 4 750 000 to the nearest million.

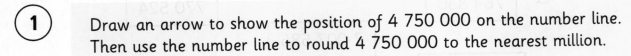

```
3 000 000        4 000 000        5 000 000
```

2 Round each number to the nearest 10 000.

573 296 [ ]   785 824 [ ]

3 Round the number shown following the instructions below.

Millions	Thousands			Ones		
O	H	T	O	H	T	O
1	4	4	9	2	5	8

To the nearest 1 000 000 [ ]

To the nearest 10 000 [ ]

To the nearest 100 [ ]

4 Circle all the numbers that round to two and a half million to the nearest hundred thousand.

2 499 875   2 521 647   2 554 361

2 448 951   2 502 128   2 549 214

5 Round the number 3 999 999 to...

... the nearest 10 000.

What do you notice?

... the nearest 100 000.

... the nearest 1 000 000.

6 The number of visitors to a theme park, rounded to the nearest hundred thousand, is three million, two hundred thousand. What are the largest and smallest possible numbers of visitors?

largest:

smallest:

Problem Solving and Reasoning

7 To be classed as an 'expert' in a computer game, you need to have a score that rounds to 7 000 000 points to the nearest million.

Eli's score is shown on the right. What is the smallest number of points he still needs to score to be classed as an 'expert'?

6 150 000

8 Isabel is thinking of a number.

What range of numbers does Isabel's number lie within?

My number rounds to 300 000 to the nearest hundred thousand, and 250 000 to the nearest ten thousand.

Are you an expert at rounding?

Negative Numbers

1 Use the number line to help you answer the questions.

$$-5 \quad -4 \quad -3 \quad -2 \quad -1 \quad 0 \quad 1 \quad 2 \quad 3 \quad 4 \quad 5$$

What is 4 more than –2? ☐   What is 7 less than 3? ☐

$-3 + 8 =$ ☐ $4 - 6 =$ ☐ $-1 - 4 =$ ☐

2 Work out the difference between each pair of numbers.

–7 and –2 ☐   –3 and 1 ☐   –4 and 5 ☐

3 On one day in January, the temperature in seven cities around the world was measured.

Use the information in the table to complete the sentences.

City	Temperature
Toronto	–3 °C
Edinburgh	1 °C
Sydney	24 °C
Beijing	–7 °C
Nairobi	22 °C
Helsinki	–6 °C
Quito	14 °C

The warmest city was ☐.

The coldest city was ☐.

The difference in temperature between Helsinki and Nairobi was ☐ °C.

☐ was 17 °C colder than Quito.

Edinburgh was 7 °C warmer than ☐.

4 Kwame parks his car in an underground car park, on floor number −3.
He takes the lift from the car park to his office, which is on the eighth floor.

How many floors up does Kwame travel in the lift?

5 Maddie counts backwards in steps of 4, starting at 9.
Circle all the numbers she will say.

Do you say the same negative numbers as positive numbers?

thirteen	six	five	four	two	one

negative one   negative three   negative five

negative seven   negative eleven   negative thirteen

6 In a science experiment, the temperature of a liquid falls by 3 °C every half an hour. The thermometer shows the temperature of the liquid at 2:30 pm.

Fill in the gaps in the table.

Time (pm)	2:00	2:30	3:00	3:30	4:00	4:30
Temperature (°C)						

10 °C
0 °C
−10 °C
−20 °C

Problem Solving and Reasoning

7 Nadiya is finding differences with negative numbers.

When do you think Nadiya's method will work and when will it give the wrong answer?

−8 and 5 have a difference of 8 + 5 = 13, so when I'm finding differences with negative numbers I can just ignore any minus signs and add the numbers.

Do you feel positive about negative numbers?

Adding and Subtracting

1 Tick the three calculations you would solve using mental methods. Then write the other calculations as column additions or subtractions on the grids.

450 000 + 5200 ☐   5437 + 2914 ☐   52 220 – 99 ☐

174 800 – 4500 ☐   84 241 – 6879 ☐

Why did you choose those calculations to do mentally?

2 Work out these additions.

```
    2  8  7  0           3  6  2  1  4  2
+   5  3  5  8        +     2  7  8  9  6
```

3 Work out these subtractions.

```
    9  6  5  4           5  5  1  0  0  5
-   4  7  3  8        -     1  4  2  3  9
```

4 Work out these calculations using column methods.

32 866 + 88 139   1 674 244 – 737 515

5 Find the missing numbers in the following calculations.

```
    [ ] 9  9 [ ] 4  2
  +   2  6 [ ] 8  4 [ ]
    ─────────────────
      7  6  7  0  8  3
```

```
      8  1  9  2 [ ]
  − [ ][ ]    1 [ ] 6
    ─────────────────
      6     1  7  8  9
```

6 The number of bricks laid by three bricklayers over ten years is shown in the table.

How many fewer bricks did Stu lay than Irena and Olek combined?

	Number of bricks
Irena	1 534 750
Olek	1 100 000
Stu	2 460 040

Problem Solving and Reasoning

7 Rachel is doing the addition 234 823 + 412 105.

Do you agree with Rachel's choice of method? Explain your answer.

> I don't need to write that down, I can do it in my head.

8 Use these bar models to work out the values of A and B.

```
       310 000
  ┌──────────────┐
  │ 190 000 │  A │
  └──────────────┘

       404 380
  ┌──────────────────┐
  │  A  │  A  │   B  │
  └──────────────────┘
```

A =

B =

Did you manage those sums?

Common Factors

1 Circle all the numbers that are in the wrong places in these sorting diagrams.

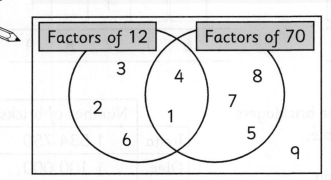

	Factor of 40	Not a factor of 40
Factor of 18	1 2 8	3 6
Not a factor of 18	4	5 7 9

2 Find all the common factors of 24 and 56.

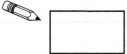

3 Find the largest number that is a factor of all the numbers in each set.

| 42 and 84 |

| 100, 150, 225 |

Problem Solving and Reasoning

4 B is a prime number and C is a different whole number.

What is the maximum number of common factors B and C could have?

Explain your answer and give an example.

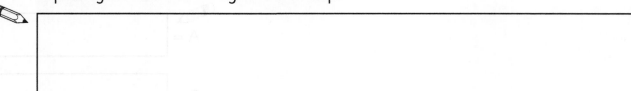

How did you find those factors?

Common Multiples

1 The number line shows some multiples of 4.

Complete the number line to show the missing multiples of 4, then circle all the numbers on the number line that are also multiples of 6.

2 List the common multiples of 3 and 8 that could go on these number lines.

3 Babar's watch beeps every 9 minutes and his phone beeps every 12 minutes. They both beep at 11:07 am. What time will they next beep together?

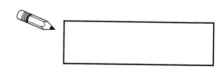

Problem Solving and Reasoning

4 Chef Chang uses a sack of carrots every 6 days and a sack of onions every 14 days. She has just opened new sacks today.

How many sacks will she have used in total from now until the next time she finishes a sack of carrots and onions on the same day?

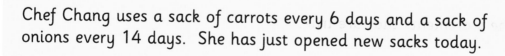
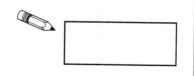

Are you a master of the multiples?

Divisibility Rules

1 Put the numbers in the box into the correct place on this sorting diagram.

	Divisible by 5	Not divisible by 5
Divisible by 2		
Not divisible by 2		

130 421
58 420
254 015
179 098

2 Using digit sums, circle the two numbers that divide exactly by 3.

4510   120 033   574 110

520 033   84 101   7708

3 List all the even 2-digit numbers that are divisible by 11.

Your answers should all be divisible by another 2-digit number. What is it and why do you think that is?

4 Tick the statements that are true.

☐ All numbers that are divisible by 9 are also divisible by 3.

☐ All numbers that are divisible by 4 are also divisible by 12.

☐ All odd numbers are divisible by 3.

☐ All numbers that are divisible by 2 and 5 are also divisible by 10.

5 A certain number can be divided by 2 three times without any remainders.

Give two whole numbers greater than 2 that the number can also definitely be divided by without giving remainders.

6 Andy needs to share 8742 peanuts evenly into bowls.

Use divisibility rules to show that he could use 6 bowls.

Problem Solving and Reasoning

7 This 7-digit number is missing some digits.
It is divisible by 5 and 9, but not divisible by 2.

7	A	2	4	1	2	B

What are the values of A and B?

A = ☐   B = ☐

8 Luke has done a division.

9871 ÷ 15 gives a remainder of 1.

Show how you can check that Luke is right using divisibility rules.

Do you know your divisibility rules? ☹ ✓ ☺ ✓ 😉 ✓

20

Prime Numbers

1 Circle all the prime numbers between 50 and 60.

51   52   53   54   55   56   57   58   59

2 Write down the prime factors of these numbers.

18 [ ]   42 [ ]

3 Complete these sentences.

The largest prime number less than 100 is [ ].

The smallest composite number is 4 because it has more than [ ] factors.

The smallest composite number greater than 80 is [ ].

Problem Solving and Reasoning

4 Complete these sums using four different prime numbers.

[ ] + [ ] = 62   [ ] + [ ] = 62

5 Charlie is thinking about prime numbers.

> There are no prime numbers that are also square numbers.

Do you agree with Charlie?
Explain your reasoning.

[ ]

Are you primed and ready to go?

Block 2 — Addition, Subtraction, Multiplication and Division — Step 5

Square and Cube Numbers

1 Here is part of a hundred square.

Shade all the square numbers and circle all the cube numbers.

21	22	23	24	25	26	27	28	29	30
31	32	33	34	35	36	37	38	39	40
41	42	43	44	45	46	47	48	49	50

2 Work out the following sums.

$8^2 + 2^3 = \boxed{}$
$4^3 - 3^2 = \boxed{}$

3 List the whole numbers that are greater than 11^2 but less than 5^3.

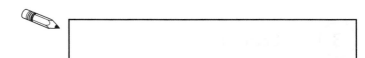

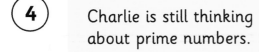
Problem Solving and Reasoning

4 Charlie is still thinking about prime numbers.

> Apart from 2 and 5, if you square a prime number, the ones digit of the result is 1 or 9.

Do you agree with Charlie this time? Explain your reasoning.

Do you know your squares and cubes?

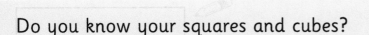

Multiplication

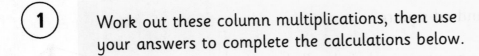

1 Work out these column multiplications, then use your answers to complete the calculations below.

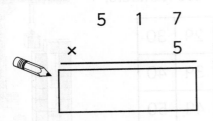

```
      5  1  7
   ×        5
   ───────────
```

```
      2  1  6  2
   ×           3
   ──────────────
```

517 × 50 = [   ]   30 × 2162 = [   ]

2 Explain what mistake has been made in the multiplication below.

```
      1  3  0  8
   ×        1  2
   ───────────────
      2  6  1₁ 6
   +  1  3  0  8
   ───────────────
      3  9  2  4
               1
```

[   ]

3 Calculate:

```
         8  3  2
   ×        1  6
   ────────────────
```

```
      5  8  0  2
   ×        3  3
   ────────────────
```

[   ]   [   ]

4 What number is 26 times bigger than 749?

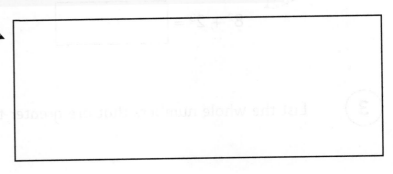

[   ]

(5) A fashion designer puts 8740 sequins on each robe they make.

How many sequins will they use on 18 robes?

> Can you think of a way to do this by only multiplying by 2 and 3?

(6) Ounces, pounds and stones are all imperial units for mass.
There are 16 ounces in 1 pound and 14 pounds in 1 stone.

How many ounces are there in 89 stone?

ounces

Problem Solving and Reasoning

(7) Mike works out that 4497 × 22 = 98 936, but he is incorrect.

How can you tell he is incorrect without doing the full calculation yourself?

(8) Look at the working out on the right carefully.

What is the missing calculation?

	?	?	?	?
×			?	?
1	3₆	1₅	3₄	9
3₁	7₁	5₁	4	0
5	0	6	7	9
1				

Got your head around multiplication?

Block 2 — Addition, Subtraction, Multiplication and Division — Step 7

Multiplication Problems

1 Complete these calculations to make both sides equal.

20 × 890 = 2 × ☐

20 × 890 = 89 × ☐

18 × 3200 = 9 × ☐

18 × 3200 = 3 × ☐ × 3200

2 Explain what is wrong with these multiplication methods.

> To multiply a number by 8, you can multiply by 4 twice.

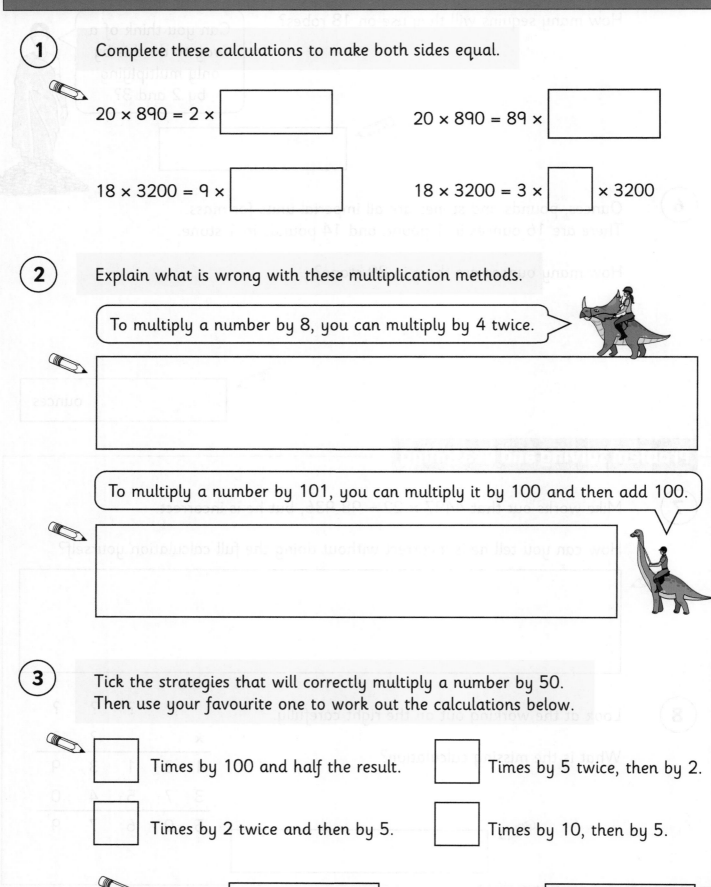

> To multiply a number by 101, you can multiply it by 100 and then add 100.

3 Tick the strategies that will correctly multiply a number by 50.
Then use your favourite one to work out the calculations below.

☐ Times by 100 and half the result.

☐ Times by 5 twice, then by 2.

☐ Times by 2 twice and then by 5.

☐ Times by 10, then by 5.

22 × 50 = ☐

46 × 50 = ☐

4 Fill in the missing numbers to work out the calculation 205 × 16.

205 × 2 = [ ]   [ ] × 2 = [ ]

[ ] × 2 = [ ]   [ ] × 2 = [ ]

5 Use an appropriate multiplication strategy to work out 340 × 99.

[ ]

Problem Solving and Reasoning

6 Calculate 241 × 9 by multiplying by three twice.

[ ]

Describe another method you could have used.

[ ]

7 Efa has a strategy for multiplying a number by 18.

> I multiply the number by 2, then I multiply the result by 10 and subtract the original number.

Do you think Efa's strategy will work? Explain your reasoning.

[ ]

Can you use multiplication strategies?

Short Division

1 Work out the values of the letters on these bar models using mental methods.

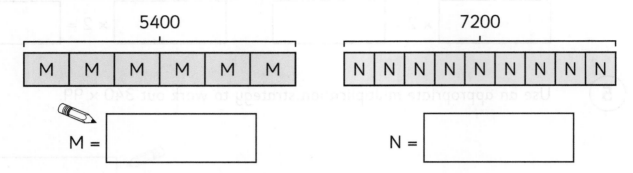

M =

N =

2 Work out these short divisions. Use the place value charts where appropriate.

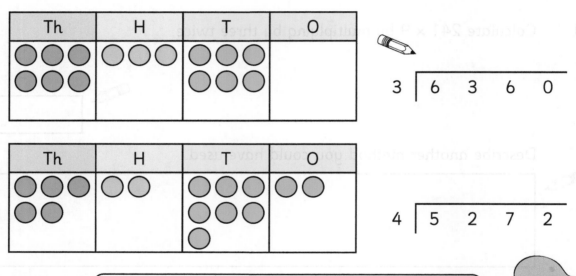

$$3 \overline{\smash{)}6\ 3\ 6\ 0}$$

$$4 \overline{\smash{)}5\ 2\ 7\ 2}$$

Are place value charts helpful in both questions?
Discuss your answer with a partner.

3 Use short division to work out:

$$5 \overline{\smash{)}4\ 3\ 1\ 5}$$

$$6 \overline{\smash{)}2\ 4\ 4\ 2}$$

$$7 \overline{\smash{)}5\ 3\ 2\ 7}$$

$$8 \overline{\smash{)}2\ 0\ 4\ 0}$$

4 A candle company packages its candles into small boxes of 4 candles or large boxes of 7 candles. They make 9740 candles.

How many small boxes can they completely fill?

How many large boxes can they completely fill?

5 A cheesecake contains 8 servings. How many cheesecakes are needed for an order of 9007 servings?

Problem Solving and Reasoning

6 A flock of sheep can be divided equally into 6, 7 or 8 pens.

Which of these could be the number of sheep? Circle the correct answer.

2394   3808   6384   8820

7 Use division to find the missing 1-digit and 2-digit numbers in this calculation. The missing 1-digit number is greater than 6.

5 × ☐ × ☐☐ = 3 4 8 0

Are you a short division pro?

Division Using Factors

1 Complete this bar model, then use it to work out the divisions below.

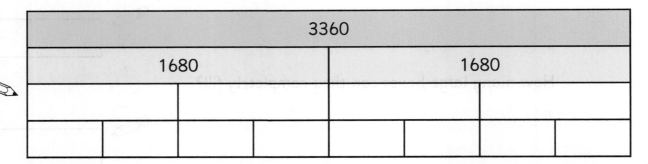

3360							
1680				1680			

3360 ÷ 4 = [   ]   3360 ÷ 8 = [   ]

2 Fill in the gaps to complete these divisions.

1740 ÷ 4 = 1740 ÷ 2 ÷ [   ] = 870 ÷ [   ] = [   ]

3606 ÷ 6 = 3606 ÷ 2 ÷ [   ] = 1803 ÷ [   ] = [   ]

3224 ÷ 8 = 3224 ÷ 2 ÷ [   ] = 1612 ÷ [   ] = [   ]

3 Tick the strategies that will correctly divide a number by 30.

[   ] Halve the number 3 times.   [   ] Divide by 10, and then by 3.

[   ] Divide by 5, and then by 6.   [   ] Divide by 5 twice, and then by 2.

4 What number do you multiply by 50 to give 5450?

[   ]

5 Circle the calculations you could do to work out 6168 ÷ 12, then choose one of them to work out the answer.

6168 ÷ 2 ÷ 6   6168 ÷ 4 ÷ 3   6168 ÷ 10 ÷ 2

6168 ÷ 3 ÷ 2   6168 ÷ 2 ÷ 2 ÷ 3   6168 ÷ 6 ÷ 3

Why did you choose that calculation?

6168 ÷ 12 = ▢

6 Jen needs to split 1568 building blocks equally into 14 boxes. She does this by splitting them into 2 groups and then splitting each group into 7 boxes.

How many blocks are there in each of the 2 groups?

▢

How many blocks are there in each of the 14 boxes?

▢

Problem Solving and Reasoning

7 Yan is trying to do division using factors.

This method isn't useful when dividing by some numbers, like 13 and 17.

Do you agree with Yan? Explain your reasoning.

▢

How were those division questions?

Block 2 — Addition, Subtraction, Multiplication and Division — Step 10

Long Division

1   Some multiples of 13 are shown on the right.

| 13 × 1 = 13 |
| 13 × 2 = 26 |
| 13 × 3 = 39 |
| 13 × 4 = 52 |
| 13 × 5 = 65 |
| 13 × 6 = 78 |
| 13 × 7 = 91 |

Use the multiples to complete these long divisions.

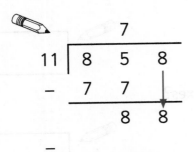

```
              2
    13 │ 3  1  2
      -  2  6  0   (13 × 20)
            5  2
      -
        _____
```

```
    13 │ 7  4  1
      -              (13 × 50)
        _____
      -
        _____
```

2   Complete these long division calculations.

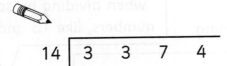

```
              7
    11 │ 8  5  8
      -  7  7  ↓
            8  8
      -
        _____
```

```
              7
    12 │ 8  7  6
      -  8  4  ↓
            3
      -
        _____
```

```
              5
    15 │ 7  6  5
      -  7  5
      -
        _____
```

3   Work out these calculations using long division.

```
    14 │ 3  3  7  4
```

```
    16 │ 5  3  1  2
```

4 What do you have to multiply 21 by to get 8925?

5 A baker's current record is to bake 8112 bagels in a day. He bakes them on trays of 13 bagels.

How many trays would he need to bake to break his record?

Would you use a different method if I made trays of 9 bagels?

Problem Solving and Reasoning

6 Why do you think someone might choose to use long division for a calculation like 2839 ÷ 17 but not for 4530 ÷ 15?

7 A sweetshop buys a jar of 4032 sweets and splits them into bags of 16 sweets. They sell all the bags for £2 each.

How much more money would they make from one jar if they split the sweets into bags of 14 but still sold the bags for £2 each?

£

Are you comfortable with long division?

Long Division with Remainders

1 Some multiples of 14 are shown on the right.

Use the multiples to complete these long divisions.

| 14 × 1 = 14 |
| 14 × 2 = 28 |
| 14 × 3 = 42 |
| 14 × 4 = 56 |
| 14 × 5 = 70 |
| 14 × 6 = 84 |
| 14 × 7 = 98 |

```
           4        r
    14 | 6   0   8
       - 5   6   0   (14 × 40)
         ─────────
           4   8
```

```
                    r
    14 | 9   1   5
       - 8   4   0   (14 × 60)
         ─────────
```

2 Work out these calculations using long division.

```
    15 | 3   5   1   4
```

```
    22 | 6   7   1   2
```

3 A hamster needs 18 g of food each day.

How many full days will a 2 kg bag of hamster food last?

How many grams would be left in the bag at the end?

days

4 2748 runners are split into groups of 62 and one smaller group.

How many runners are in the smaller group?

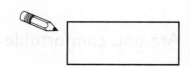

5 A company has £6738 to divide equally
between 12 departments for food and drink.

How much will each department get?

£

Problem Solving and Reasoning

6 Without doing the calculation, do you think that
7845 ÷ 18 will give a remainder? Explain your answer.

7 A luxury yacht can transport 24 passengers to an island in one trip.

How many trips would they have to make to transport 3851 passengers?

> If the luxury yacht was half full each time,
> we would have to do twice as many trips.

Do you agree? Explain your reasoning.

Do you know how to handle remainders?

Division Problems

1 Sort these divisions into the table to show the most appropriate method to solve them.

| 858 ÷ 7 | 2844 ÷ 6 | 1357 ÷ 59 | 2400 ÷ 8 |
| 999 ÷ 3 | 7482 ÷ 4 | 9482 ÷ 14 | 8800 ÷ 22 |

Short Division	Long Division	Mental Method

2 Solve these divisions by completing the partition diagrams.

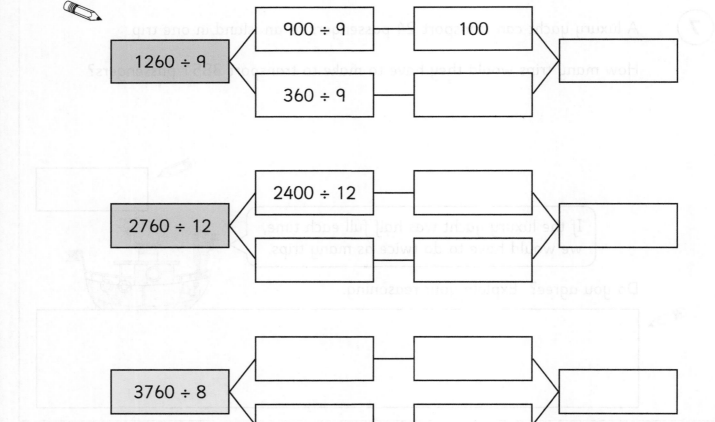

1260 ÷ 9 → 900 ÷ 9 → 100

360 ÷ 9 →

2760 ÷ 12 → 2400 ÷ 12 →

3760 ÷ 8 →

3 Asafa is laying tiles in rows of 9. He has laid 725 tiles so far.

How many full rows has he laid?

4 At a theme park, a ride on the pirate ship is either 3 loops or 7 swings.

The pirate ship is repainted after it has done 327 loops and 469 swings. How many rides is this?

Try doing the questions above again using a different method of division. Do you get the same answers? Which method do you think is best?

Problem Solving and Reasoning

5 One strategy to divide a 4-digit number by a 1-digit number mentally is shown here.

$8154 \div 9$
$8100 \div 9 = 900 \quad 54 \div 9 = 6$
$900 + 6 = \mathbf{906}$

Use the strategy to do these divisions mentally.

$6448 \div 8$ $6307 \div 7$

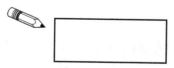   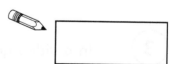

Do you think this is always a good strategy to use? Explain your reasoning.

Are you confident with dividing?

Multi-Step Calculation Problems

1 At a stationery shop, calculators cost £8 and geometry sets cost £4.
A teacher buys 180 calculators and 90 geometry sets.

Circle the calculation that works out the total cost in pounds.
Then use the calculation to find the total cost.

$(180 + 90) \times (8 - 4)$ $(8 + 4) \times (180 - 90)$

$(4 \times 90) + (8 \times 180)$ $(180 \times 8) - (90 \times 4)$

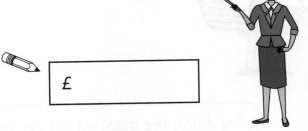

Can you write the correct calculation as a single multiplication?

£

2 At a stadium, there are 25 sections of seats.
Each section has 14 rows and each row has 10 seats.

How many more seats are needed for the stadium to have 5200 seats?

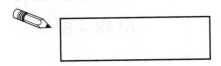

3 In a video game, a player gets 1650 points for completing each level.
They get an extra 200 points for completing the level within the time limit.

How many points would a player get for completing
12 levels in total and 5 within the time limit?

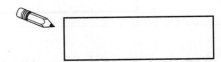

4 A sports event charges £39 for an adult ticket and £19 for a child ticket. They have sold 200 adult tickets, and have taken over £10 000 in total.

What is the smallest number of child tickets they could have sold?

Problem Solving and Reasoning

5 A book has 8 chapters and 3784 words. Each chapter has the same number of pages and each page has the same number of words.

Could each chapter be made up of 3 pages? Explain your reasoning.

6 Look at the bar model below.

12 439					
8789					
920	A				

What is the value of A?

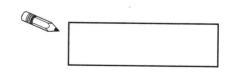

How did you find those problems?

Order of Operations

1 Label these operations 1-4 to show the order in which you should do them in a calculation.

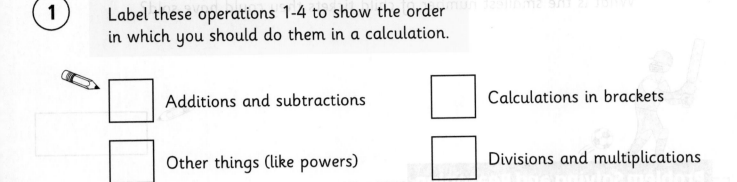

☐ Additions and subtractions

☐ Calculations in brackets

☐ Other things (like powers)

☐ Divisions and multiplications

2 Work out these calculations.

$5 + 2 \times 6 =$ ☐

$15 \div 5 - 2 =$ ☐

$(8 + 12) \div 4 =$ ☐

$12 \times (3 - 3) =$ ☐

3 Circle the calculations where the answer would not change if you removed the brackets.

$3^2 + (3 \times 3)$ $9 - (5 - 3)$ $(60 \div 5) + 7$

$50 \times (4 - 1)$ $(40 + 8) \div 2$ $80 \div (5 + 3)$

4 At a party, 20 guests are outside. Half of them leave. 8 guests are inside and 2 of them leave.

Write a single calculation that could be used to work out how many guests are still at the party.

You can use brackets here, but do you need to?

5 Fill in the correct symbol (<, > or =) between each pair of calculations.

$7 + 5 \times 3$ ☐ $30 - 8 \div 2$ $(5 + 4) \times (8 - 3)$ ☐ $40 + 10 \div 2$

$7 - 3 \times 2 + 4$ ☐ $2 \times 2 - 1$ $18 - 12 \div 2$ ☐ $2 \times 8 - 2^2$

6 Write any of the four operations (+, −, ×, ÷) in each gap to correctly complete these calculations.

8 ☐ 4 ☐ $3 = -1$ 9 ☐ 5 ☐ 7 ☐ $9 = 77$

Problem Solving and Reasoning

7 Don is doing a calculation.

Do you agree with Don? Explain your answer.

> To do 15 − 8 + 5, I should do the addition first to give 15 − 13 and then do the subtraction to give 2.

8 Look at the calculation $20 - 4 \times 3 + 2$.

By putting in one pair of brackets, what is the largest answer you can make?

By putting in one pair of brackets, what is the smallest answer you can make?

Have you got your operations in order?   ✓   ✓   ✓

Estimating and Mental Maths

1 Circle the calculations that would be sensible to do when estimating.

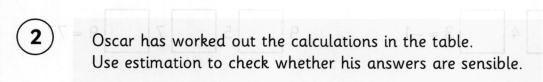

6000 ÷ 20	67 800 + 54 900

| 8000 × 68 | 89 000 − 4000 |

| 9000 + 200 000 | 41 100 − 19 200 |

Why did you choose each of those calculations?

2 Oscar has worked out the calculations in the table.
Use estimation to check whether his answers are sensible.

Calculation	Estimation	Is it sensible?
4138 × 19 = 62 622		Yes / No
2868 + 3916 = 6784		Yes / No
3822 ÷ 98 = 39		Yes / No

3 Work out these calculations using mental strategies.

570 + 97 + 130

40 × 8 × 50

(120 + 99) ÷ 3

4 Louise walks 72 km every month.

Estimate how far she walks in a year, then complete the sentence below using "shorter" or "longer".

km

My estimate is [ ] than the actual distance Louise walks.

5 One serving of cereal is 38.5 g.

Estimate how many servings are in three 800 g boxes.

Problem Solving and Reasoning

6 Kai is estimating a calculation.

Do you agree with Kai?
Explain your reasoning.

> If I round all the numbers up, then the estimation will be bigger than the actual answer.

7 Look at the three estimations for the calculation 8752 × 34.

Which estimation do you think is best?
What is wrong with the other estimations?

| 9000 × 30 = 270 000 |
| 8000 × 30 = 240 000 |
| 9000 × 34 = 306 000 |

Did you manage those in your head?

Using Known Facts

1 Use the calculation shown to complete three more calculations using the same numbers.

$$3285 + 2947 = 6232$$

☐ + ☐ = ☐

☐ − ☐ = ☐

☐ − ☐ = ☐

2 Represent each of these calculations on the bar models given.

$$57\,800 - 35\,900 = 21\,900$$

$$872 \div 4 = 218$$

3 Fill in the missing numbers in these additions and subtractions.

$7485 + 495 = 500 +$ ☐

$9420 - 498 =$ ☐ $- 500$

$988 + 327 =$ ☐ $+ 1000$

$179 + 648 = 180 + 650 -$ ☐

4 Circle all the calculations that will have the same answer as 170×50.

340×100 340×25 $5 \times 10 \times 170$

17×5000 85×100 $200 \times 50 - 30$

5 Use the area model to put these calculations in order of size, starting with the smallest answer. Then complete the calculations below.

52   1

41   2132

1

53 × 42   52 × 41   53 × 41   52 × 42

[   ]   [   ]   [   ]   [   ]

smallest   largest

52 × 42 = [   ]   53 × 42 = [   ]

6 Use the fact in the box to fill in the missing numbers.   68 × 32 = 2176

680 × 320 = 2176 × [   ] = [   ]

78 × 32 = 2176 + [   ] = [   ]

2176 ÷ 16 = 2176 ÷ 32 × [   ] = [   ] × [   ] = [   ]

Problem Solving and Reasoning

7 ● and ▲ are both positive whole numbers. Use the fact that ● × ▲ = 4590 to tick the statement below which **must** be true.

[ ] Either ● or ▲ is divisible by 10.

[ ] If you add 10 to ● and subtract 1 from ▲ then multiply those numbers, it will be bigger than 4590.

[ ] Either ● or ▲ is divisible by 5.

[ ] Both ● and ▲ have a factor of 3.

Explain your choice to a partner and see if they agree.

How are your reasoning skills?   ☑ ☑ ☑

Block 3 — Fractions A

Equivalent Fractions

(1) Fill in the missing numerators and denominators to complete these sentences.

$\dfrac{3}{6}$ is equivalent to $\dfrac{1}{\boxed{}}$ and $\dfrac{5}{\boxed{}}$.

$\dfrac{6}{8}$ is equivalent to $\dfrac{\boxed{}}{4}$ and $\dfrac{\boxed{}}{12}$.

(2) Circle all the fractions that are equivalent to $\dfrac{1}{3}$.

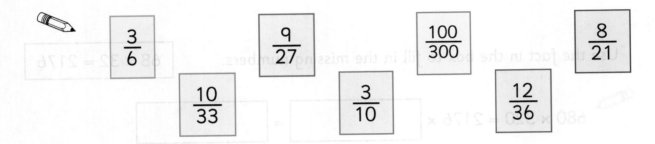

$\dfrac{3}{6}$ $\dfrac{9}{27}$ $\dfrac{100}{300}$ $\dfrac{8}{21}$

$\dfrac{10}{33}$ $\dfrac{3}{10}$ $\dfrac{12}{36}$

(3) Write each fraction in its simplest form.

$\dfrac{6}{14} = \boxed{}$ $\dfrac{10}{55} = \boxed{}$ $\dfrac{13}{26} = \boxed{}$

How do you know if the fraction is <u>fully</u> simplified?

$\dfrac{18}{30} = \boxed{}$ $\dfrac{24}{28} = \boxed{}$ $\dfrac{60}{144} = \boxed{}$

(4) Using only numbers up to 100 on the numerator and denominator, list all the different fractions you can find that are equivalent to $\dfrac{5}{12}$.

5 Fill in the boxes to show the fully simplified mixed numbers.

$2\frac{4}{6} = \boxed{}\frac{2}{\boxed{}}$

$\frac{30}{24} = \frac{5}{\boxed{}} = \boxed{}\frac{1}{\boxed{}}$

$4\frac{18}{21} = \boxed{}\frac{\boxed{}}{7}$

$\frac{24}{10} = \boxed{}\frac{\boxed{}}{10} = \boxed{}\frac{\boxed{}}{5}$

Problem Solving and Reasoning

6 Aaron and Monifa have tried to fully simplify $4\frac{8}{12}$, but both have got the wrong answer. Explain what each child has done wrong.

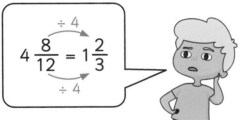

7 Isak claims that there are 33 fractions equivalent to $\frac{2}{3}$ (including $\frac{2}{3}$ itself) where the denominator is a whole number less than 100.

Do you agree with Isak? Explain how you know.

How simple did you find those fractions?

Equivalent Fractions on Number Lines

1 Write each fraction shown on the number line in its simplest form.

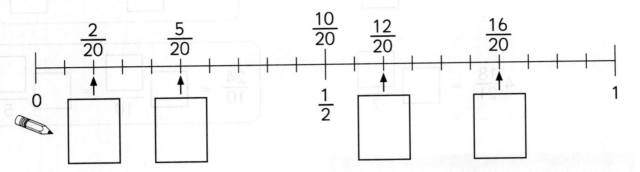

2 Draw lines to match each shape to the label on the number line that shows what fraction of the shape is shaded.

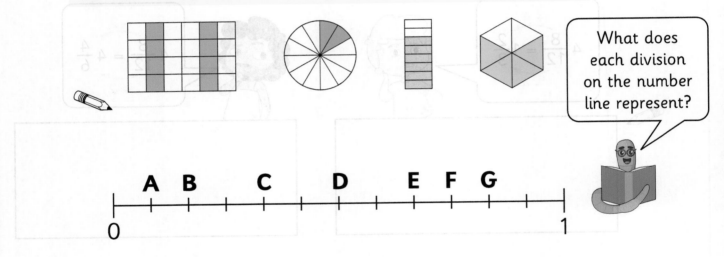

What does each division on the number line represent?

3 Divide the bar model into the fractions below, working in order from A to F. One has been done for you.

$A = \dfrac{1}{8}$ $B = \dfrac{1}{2}$ $C = 1$ whole $D = \dfrac{1}{4}$ $E = \dfrac{3}{4}$ $F = \dfrac{3}{8}$

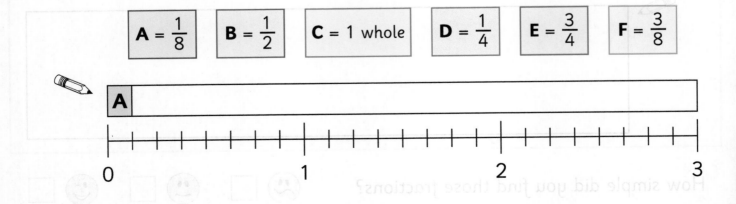

4 Write the letter that shows each fraction's position on the number line.

A B   C D   E   F G

0   1   2   3

$2\frac{2}{10} = \boxed{}$
$\frac{7}{5} = \boxed{}$
$1\frac{80}{100} = \boxed{}$
$\frac{18}{30} = \boxed{}$

5 Draw lines to show where these fractions go on the number line below.

$\frac{1}{8}$
$\frac{150}{100}$
$\frac{45}{40}$
$1\frac{14}{16}$
$\frac{33}{66}$

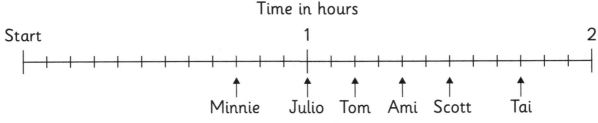

0   1   2

Problem Solving and Reasoning

6 The timeline shows when some children finished a treasure hunt.

Time in hours

Start   1   2

Minnie   Julio Tom Ami Scott   Tai

Who took $1\frac{1}{3}$ hours to finish?

$\boxed{}$

Jada finished halfway between Minnie and Julio.
What fraction of an hour did she take? Explain your answer.

How did you get on with those questions? ✓ ✓ ✓

Ordering Fractions using Denominators

1 Shade the bar models to show each fraction, then fill in the correct symbol (< or >) to make the comparisons correct.

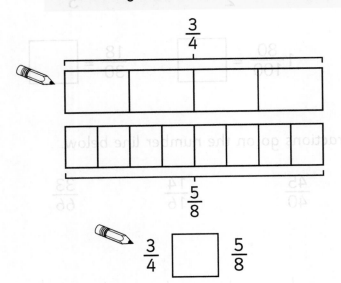

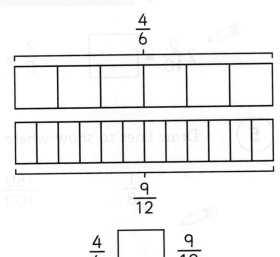

$\frac{3}{4}$ [ ] $\frac{5}{8}$ $\frac{4}{6}$ [ ] $\frac{9}{12}$

2 Write < or > in each box to make the comparison correct.

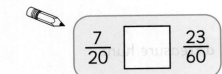 $\frac{7}{20}$ [ ] $\frac{23}{60}$ $\frac{19}{24}$ [ ] $\frac{3}{4}$ $\frac{9}{13}$ [ ] $\frac{19}{26}$

3 Circle the larger number in each box.

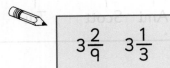 $3\frac{2}{9}$ $3\frac{1}{3}$ $8\frac{4}{5}$ $8\frac{3}{4}$ $2\frac{5}{8}$ $\frac{11}{4}$ $\frac{19}{6}$ $3\frac{3}{10}$

4 Write these fractions with a common denominator to work out which is the smallest.

$\frac{7}{25}$ = [ ] $\frac{2}{5}$ = [ ] $\frac{3}{10}$ = [ ]

The smallest fraction is: [ ]

5 Put these fractions in order from smallest to largest.

$$\frac{2}{3} \qquad \frac{3}{5} \qquad \frac{5}{6} \qquad \frac{7}{10} \qquad \frac{11}{15}$$

Smallest ⟶ Largest

6 Without finding equivalent fractions, circle the larger fraction below.

$$\frac{301}{300} \qquad \text{or} \qquad \frac{749}{750}$$

Explain how you know.

Problem Solving and Reasoning

7 Three children are eating apples.

Maura cuts her apple into 8 equal slices and eats 7 of them.
Noor cuts her apple into 12 equal slices and eats 9 of them.
Phil cuts his apple into 6 equal slices and eats 5 of them.

Who ate the most of their apple? Who ate the least?

Most ⟶ Least

8 Circle the fractions below that would appear on the number line.

$$\frac{7}{10} \qquad\qquad\qquad\qquad \frac{9}{10}$$

$$\frac{4}{5} \qquad \frac{99}{100} \qquad \frac{789}{1000} \qquad \frac{49}{60} \qquad \frac{27}{40} \qquad \frac{23}{25}$$

Can you compare and order fractions?

Ordering Fractions using Numerators

1 Split the circle on the right into 8 equal parts, then use the circles to work out whether $\frac{1}{6}$ or $\frac{1}{8}$ is bigger.

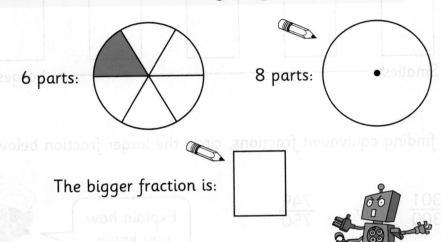

6 parts: 8 parts:

The bigger fraction is: ☐

2 Write < or > in each box to make the comparison correct.

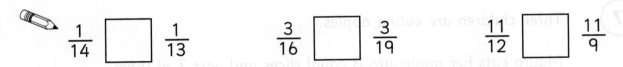

$\frac{1}{14}$ ☐ $\frac{1}{13}$ $\frac{3}{16}$ ☐ $\frac{3}{19}$ $\frac{11}{12}$ ☐ $\frac{11}{9}$

3 Circle the larger fraction in each box.

$\frac{1}{7}$ $\frac{2}{15}$ $\frac{5}{22}$ $\frac{1}{5}$ $\frac{2}{11}$ $\frac{3}{16}$ $\frac{6}{13}$ $\frac{4}{9}$

4 By writing the improper fractions as mixed numbers, work out which one is the smallest.

$\frac{34}{11} = $ ☐ $\frac{40}{13} = $ ☐ $\frac{28}{9} = $ ☐

The smallest fraction is: ☐

5 Write the fractions in the box in order from smallest to largest.

$\frac{2}{9}$ $\frac{6}{29}$ $\frac{1}{5}$ $\frac{3}{11}$

6 Make each statement correct by writing < or > in the box.

$\frac{13}{14}$ ☐ $\frac{12}{13}$ $\frac{15}{16}$ ☐ $\frac{18}{19}$ $\frac{11}{12}$ ☐ $\frac{8}{9}$

Which fraction in Q6 is closest to 1?

Problem Solving and Reasoning

7 Jon has some blocks and some cubes. He stacks 12 blocks into one tower, and 21 cubes into a second tower. The two towers are the same height.

Which is taller, one block or two cubes? Explain how you know.

8 Use the digits 3, 5, 7 and 9 once each to fill in the boxes so that the comparisons are correct.

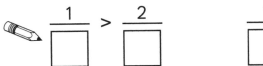 $\frac{1}{\square} > \frac{2}{\square}$ $\frac{1}{\square} < \frac{2}{\square}$

Is there more than one correct option for either of the comparisons?

Did you find that topic tricky?   ✓   ✓   ✓

Adding and Subtracting Simple Fractions

1 Fill in the boxes to make the additions and subtractions correct.

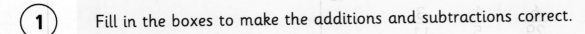

$$\frac{1}{7} + \frac{2}{7} = \frac{\boxed{}}{7}$$

$$\frac{9}{13} - \frac{\boxed{}}{13} = \frac{7}{13}$$

$$\frac{\boxed{}}{11} + \frac{8}{11} = 1\frac{2}{11}$$

2 $\frac{5}{12}$ of a drink is mango juice, and $\frac{1}{3}$ is pineapple juice.
The rest is orange juice.

How much of the drink is orange juice?
Use the diagram to help you.

3 Use equivalent fractions to work out these calculations.
Give each answer in its simplest form.

$$\frac{4}{5} - \frac{1}{10} = \boxed{}$$

$$\frac{5}{18} + \frac{1}{2} = \boxed{}$$

$$\frac{3}{40} + \frac{3}{8} = \boxed{}$$

$$\frac{6}{7} - \frac{40}{49} = \boxed{}$$

$$\frac{5}{12} + \frac{19}{60} + \frac{4}{15} = \boxed{}$$

Problem Solving and Reasoning

4 A bag contains red, blue, green and yellow balls.

Red and blue balls make up $\frac{9}{16}$ of the bag.

Red and green balls make up $\frac{1}{2}$ of the bag.

$\frac{3}{16}$ of the balls in the bag are red.

What fraction of the balls are yellow?
Give your answer in its simplest form.

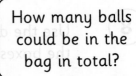

How many balls could be in the bag in total?

How did you get on with that page?

Adding and Subtracting Any Fractions

1 Work out these calculations by find the smallest common denominator.

The smallest common denominator for 5ths and 7ths is:  ☐

$\frac{1}{7} + \frac{2}{5} =$ ☐ $\frac{1}{5} + \frac{4}{7} =$ ☐ $\frac{6}{7} - \frac{3}{5} =$ ☐ $\frac{4}{5} - \frac{2}{7} =$ ☐

2 Fill in the missing fractions in these bar models.

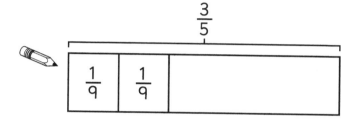

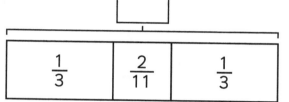

3 Circle the calculation that has the largest answer.

$\frac{59}{72} - \frac{1}{4}$ $\frac{7}{36} + \frac{3}{8}$ $\frac{8}{9} - \frac{5}{24}$ $\frac{1}{8} + \frac{7}{18}$

Problem Solving and Reasoning

4 Ceara has tried to add some fractions. Here is her working out:

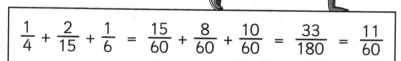

$\frac{1}{4} + \frac{2}{15} + \frac{1}{6} = \frac{15}{60} + \frac{8}{60} + \frac{10}{60} = \frac{33}{180} = \frac{11}{60}$

Explain what she has done wrong, and find the right answer in its simplest form.

Are you on the way to being a fraction pro?

54

Adding Mixed Numbers

1 Work out these additions. Use the bar models to help you.

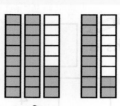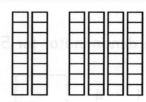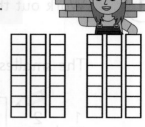

$2\frac{3}{8} + 1\frac{2}{8} =$ ☐

$1\frac{5}{8} + 3\frac{4}{8} =$ ☐

$2\frac{7}{8} + 2\frac{3}{4} =$ ☐

2 Add these mixed numbers. Give each answer as a mixed number in its simplest form.

$2\frac{4}{9} + 1\frac{2}{9} =$ ☐

$10\frac{3}{10} + 1\frac{1}{5} =$ ☐

$5\frac{1}{8} + 2\frac{1}{4} =$ ☐

$1\frac{1}{12} + 1\frac{5}{6} =$ ☐

$3\frac{2}{5} + 2\frac{1}{7} =$ ☐

$2\frac{3}{4} + 2\frac{5}{9} =$ ☐

Problem Solving and Reasoning

3 Beth wants to fit some books from a series on a shelf that is 10 cm wide. She starts with Book 1 and puts them on the shelf in order.

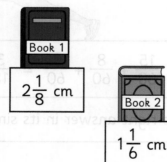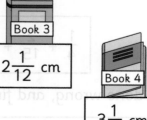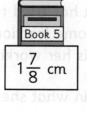

Book 1 $2\frac{1}{8}$ cm

Book 2 $1\frac{1}{6}$ cm

Book 3 $2\frac{1}{12}$ cm

Book 4 $3\frac{1}{2}$ cm

Book 5 $1\frac{7}{8}$ cm

Book 6 $1\frac{3}{4}$ cm

What is the last book that will fit on the shelf before she runs out of room?

Book ☐

Did you have 'sum' fun with this page?

Block 3 — Fractions A — Step 7

Subtracting Mixed Numbers

1 Work out the answers to these subtractions in their simplest form.

$2\frac{5}{6} - 1\frac{1}{6} =$ ⬚ $4\frac{8}{15} - 3\frac{7}{15} =$ ⬚ $5\frac{4}{5} - 2\frac{3}{10} =$ ⬚

2 Complete these subtractions. Give each answer in its simplest form.

$2\frac{1}{8} - 1\frac{1}{4} =$ ⬚ $8\frac{1}{2} - 5\frac{3}{13} =$ ⬚

$7\frac{1}{12} - 4\frac{7}{9} =$ ⬚

What do you need to do if the subtraction goes across a whole?

3 Fill in the missing fractions in the bar models.

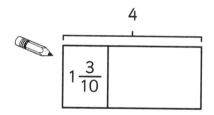

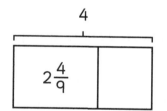

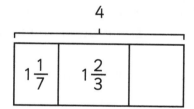

Problem Solving and Reasoning

4 Each step on the number line below is the same size. Work out where the number line starts.

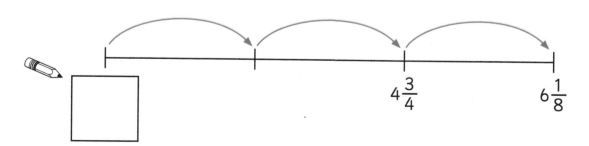

$4\frac{3}{4}$ $6\frac{1}{8}$

How did you find those questions?

Multi-Step Fraction Problems

1 Val has some bottles of apple, orange and grape juice.

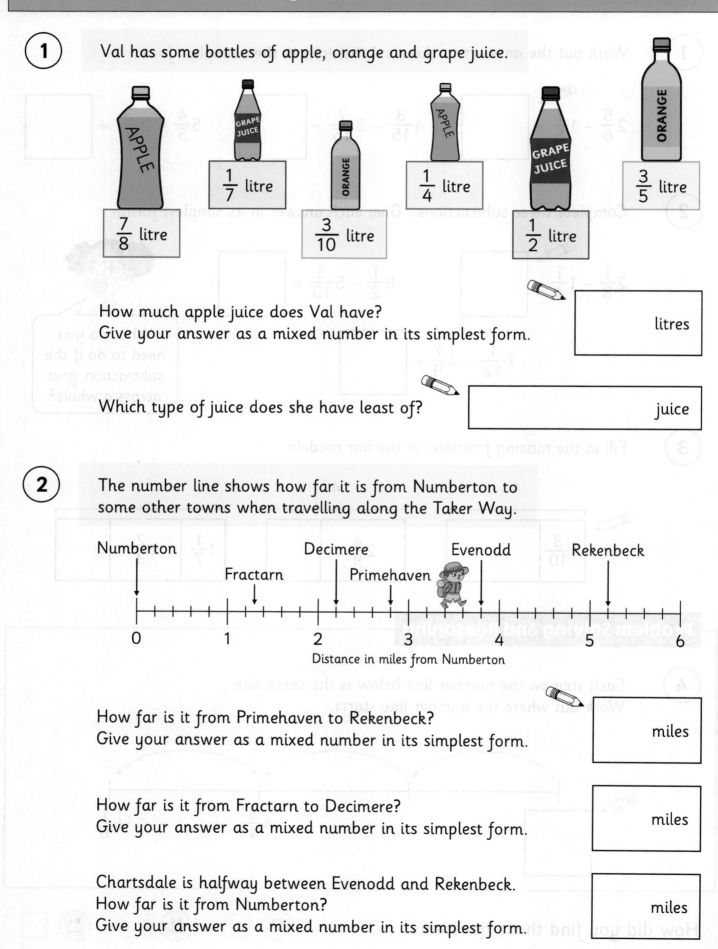

APPLE $\frac{7}{8}$ litre

GRAPE JUICE $\frac{1}{7}$ litre

ORANGE $\frac{3}{10}$ litre

APPLE $\frac{1}{4}$ litre

GRAPE JUICE $\frac{1}{2}$ litre

ORANGE $\frac{3}{5}$ litre

How much apple juice does Val have?
Give your answer as a mixed number in its simplest form.

litres

Which type of juice does she have least of?

juice

2 The number line shows how far it is from Numberton to some other towns when travelling along the Taker Way.

Numberton   Fractarn   Decimere   Primehaven   Evenodd   Rekenbeck

0   1   2   3   4   5   6

Distance in miles from Numberton

How far is it from Primehaven to Rekenbeck?
Give your answer as a mixed number in its simplest form.

miles

How far is it from Fractarn to Decimere?
Give your answer as a mixed number in its simplest form.

miles

Chartsdale is halfway between Evenodd and Rekenbeck.
How far is it from Numberton?
Give your answer as a mixed number in its simplest form.

miles

(3) Sumi made a pizza for her friends.

Sumi had $\frac{1}{6}$ of the pizza.

Pierre had $\frac{5}{33}$ of the pizza.

  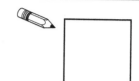

Jack had $\frac{2}{11}$ of the pizza.

Hannah had as much as Sumi and Pierre combined.

Fatma had the rest of the pizza.
How much of the pizza did Fatma eat?

Problem Solving and Reasoning

(4)

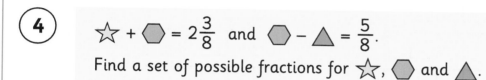

$\bigstar + \hexagon = 2\frac{3}{8}$ and $\hexagon - \triangle = \frac{5}{8}$.

Find a set of possible fractions for $\bigstar$, $\hexagon$ and $\triangle$.

What methods can you use to find an answer? Ask a friend what they did.

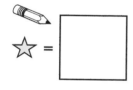 $\bigstar = $ [ ]   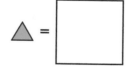 $\hexagon = $ [ ] $\triangle = $ [ ]

(5) Complete the bar model. Give all your fractions in their simplest form and give any numbers greater than 1 as mixed numbers.

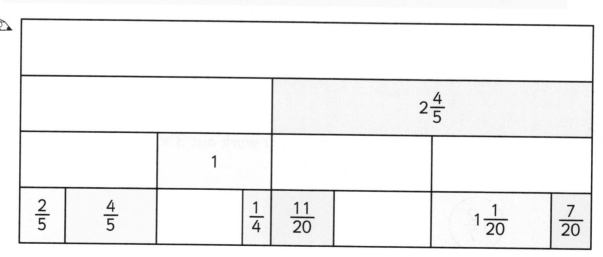

					$2\frac{4}{5}$		
		1					
$\frac{2}{5}$	$\frac{4}{5}$		$\frac{1}{4}$	$\frac{11}{20}$		$1\frac{1}{20}$	$\frac{7}{20}$

How are your fraction skills shaping up?

Multiplying Fractions by Whole Numbers

1   Write out $3 \times \frac{3}{4}$ as a repeated addition.
Then find the answer as a mixed number.

2   Work out these multiplications. Use the bar models to help you.
Give your answers as mixed numbers.

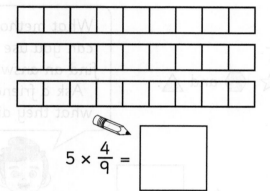

$5 \times \frac{4}{9} =$

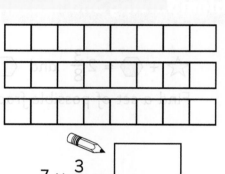

$7 \times \frac{3}{8} =$

3   Work out these multiplications. Give your answers
as improper fractions in their simplest form.

$8 \times \frac{3}{10} =$

$\frac{5}{6} \times 3 =$

$4 \times \frac{7}{12} =$

4   Use the part-whole model to help you work out $3 \times 1\frac{2}{7}$.
Give your answer as a mixed number.

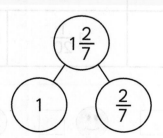

(5) Work out the answers to these multiplications.
Give your answers as mixed numbers in their simplest form.

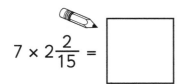

$7 \times 2\frac{2}{15} =$ ⬚

$3 \times 4\frac{5}{12} =$ ⬚

> You can convert to improper fractions first, or use partitioning. Which method do you prefer?

(6) A smoothie bottle holds $2\frac{4}{5}$ litres of smoothie. A cafe uses 4 bottles a day.
How much smoothie do they use each day?

_____ litres

(7) Shona is making cupcakes. She uses $\frac{5}{8}$ of a banana to decorate each cupcake. How many bananas will she need to decorate 160 cupcakes?

⬚

Problem Solving and Reasoning

(8) Imran, Tilly and Samira each try to calculate $3 \times 4\frac{2}{7}$.
Who has got the correct answer? What mistakes have the others made?

Imran:

$3 \times 4\frac{2}{7} = 4\frac{6}{7}$

Tilly:

$3 \times 4\frac{2}{7} = 12\frac{6}{21}$

Samira:

$3 \times 4\frac{2}{7} = 12\frac{6}{7}$

How did you get on with this step?

Multiplying Fractions by Fractions

1 Colour $\frac{1}{2}$ of the shape below yellow, then colour $\frac{1}{5}$ of the yellow part blue. Use the shape to help you work out $\frac{1}{2} \times \frac{1}{5}$.

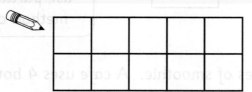

$\frac{1}{2} \times \frac{1}{5} = \boxed{}$

> Are your answers bigger or smaller than the fractions you've multiplied? Why do you think this is?

2 Work out:

$\frac{1}{3} \times \frac{1}{4} = \boxed{}$ $\frac{1}{5} \times \frac{1}{8} = \boxed{}$ $\frac{1}{6} \times \frac{1}{10} = \boxed{}$

3 Work out the following multiplications, giving your answers in their simplest form.

$\frac{1}{2} \times \frac{2}{9} = \boxed{}$ $\frac{2}{3} \times \frac{3}{4} = \boxed{}$ $\frac{3}{8} \times \frac{5}{6} = \boxed{}$

Problem Solving and Reasoning

4 A museum is divided into five areas of the same size. Three of the areas are used for exhibitions. An exhibit on Vikings takes up $\frac{5}{8}$ of the exhibition space, and an exhibit on Ancient Egypt takes up the rest of the exhibition space.

What fraction of the whole museum is taken up by the exhibit on Ancient Egypt?

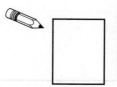 

Can you multiply fractions by other fractions?

Dividing Fractions by Whole Numbers

1 Work out these divisions. Use the bar models to help you.

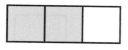

$\frac{2}{3} \div 2 =$ ☐

$\frac{4}{5} \div 4 =$ ☐

$\frac{3}{7} \div 3 =$ ☐

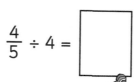 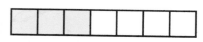
What do you notice?

2 Work out these divisions. Use the diagrams to help you.

$\frac{6}{8} \div 2 =$ ☐

$\frac{8}{9} \div 4 =$ ☐

$\frac{9}{10} \div 3 =$ ☐

3 Calculate:

$\frac{5}{12} \div 5 =$ ☐

$\frac{7}{20} \div 7 =$ ☐

$\frac{12}{15} \div 3 =$ ☐

$\frac{18}{25} \div 6 =$ ☐

4 Kesia uses $\frac{9}{20}$ of a bag of flour to make 3 pies. She uses the same amount of flour in each pie.

What fraction of the bag of flour does she use in each pie?

5 Work out these divisions. Use the diagrams to help you.

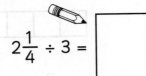

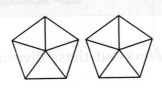

$2\frac{1}{4} \div 3 =$

$1\frac{3}{5} \div 4 =$

6 By first writing the mixed numbers as improper fractions, calculate:

$2\frac{2}{9} \div 10 =$ $\div 10 =$

$4\frac{1}{8} \div 11 =$ $\div 11 =$

7 Work out:

$2\frac{7}{10} \div 3 =$

$4\frac{1}{5} \div 7 =$

$2\frac{11}{12} \div 5 =$

Problem Solving and Reasoning

8 Kyle divides a mixed number by 5 and gets the answer $\frac{7}{8}$.
What mixed number did he start with?

Is your answer the only mixed number Kyle could have started with?

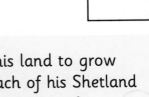

9 Farmer Faizal has $5\frac{1}{4}$ acres of land. He uses one third of his land to grow cabbages. The rest is split equally into two fields, one for each of his Shetland ponies Winston and Gloria (who don't get on so need their own space).

How big is Gloria's field?
Give your answer as a mixed number.

acres

Can you divide fractions with confidence?

More on Dividing Fractions by Whole Numbers

1 Use the diagrams to help you do these divisions.

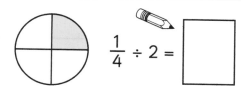 $\frac{1}{4} \div 2 =$ ☐

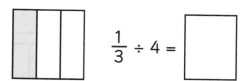 $\frac{1}{3} \div 4 =$ ☐

2 By first finding an equivalent fraction, work out:

$\frac{1}{6} \div 3 =$ ☐ $\div 3 =$ ☐

What changes?
What stays the same?

3 Calculate:

$\frac{1}{8} \div 2 =$ ☐

$\frac{5}{12} \div 3 =$ ☐

$\frac{3}{10} \div 5 =$ ☐

4 Fill in the missing numbers.

$\frac{1}{5} \div$ ☐ $= \frac{1}{20}$

$\frac{3}{4} \div$ ☐ $= \frac{3}{28}$

$\frac{2}{9} \div$ ☐ $= \frac{2}{45}$

Problem Solving and Reasoning

5 Pip has a jar of apricot jam, which is $\frac{2}{3}$ full, and an identically-sized jar of plum jam, which is $\frac{3}{5}$ full. He divides all of his apricot jam equally between 10 slices of toast, and all of his plum jam equally between 6 slices of toast.

Is there more jam on a slice of toast with apricot jam
or a slice of toast with plum jam?

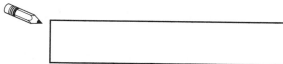

How did you find these trickier divisions?

Mixed Fractions Questions

1 Circle the bar model that shows the calculation $\frac{1}{4} + \frac{2}{5} \times 4$.

?

| $\frac{1}{4}$ | $\frac{2}{5}$ | $\frac{2}{5}$ | $\frac{2}{5}$ | $\frac{2}{5}$ |

?

| $\frac{1}{4}$ | $\frac{2}{5}$ | $\frac{1}{4}$ | $\frac{2}{5}$ | $\frac{1}{4}$ | $\frac{2}{5}$ | $\frac{1}{4}$ | $\frac{2}{5}$ |

2 Draw lines to match each problem to the calculation you would have to do to find the amount of liquid in each cup.

Tamsin has $\frac{3}{5}$ of a litre of lemonade.
She shares it equally between three cups.

$\boxed{\dfrac{3}{5} - \dfrac{3}{10}}$

Leah mixes $\frac{3}{10}$ of a litre of coconut water
with $\frac{1}{5}$ of a litre of pineapple juice in a cup.

$\boxed{3 \times \dfrac{1}{5}}$

Sebastian has $\frac{3}{5}$ of a litre of water in a cup.
He pours $\frac{3}{10}$ of a litre away.

$\boxed{\dfrac{3}{5} \div 3}$

Kofi has three 1-litre bottles of fruit juice.
He pours $\frac{1}{5}$ of each bottle into a cup.

$\boxed{\dfrac{3}{10} + \dfrac{1}{5}}$

3 Circle the calculation that has the smallest answer.

$\boxed{\dfrac{1}{3} \times \dfrac{5}{8}}$ $\boxed{\dfrac{3}{8} + \dfrac{1}{12}}$ $\boxed{\dfrac{7}{12} \div 2}$ $\boxed{2\dfrac{1}{6} - 1\dfrac{7}{8}}$

4 Mr Evans is making cereal for his family's breakfast.
He mixes $\frac{1}{2}$ kg of oats, $\frac{2}{9}$ kg of dried fruit and $\frac{1}{6}$ kg of nuts
together, then shares the mixture evenly between 4 bowls.

What mass of cereal is in each bowl?
Give your answer as a fraction in its simplest form.

	kg

**5** Find the answers to the following calculations, giving your answers in their simplest form and as mixed numbers where needed.

$$\left(\frac{1}{8} + \frac{2}{5}\right) \div 3 =$$

$$3\frac{1}{5} \times 2 + \frac{3}{20} =$$

6 A fair is taking place on a school field. $\frac{23}{50}$ of the field is being used for stalls, and the rest of the field is split equally between games and seating. There are 9 game zones, and each one takes up the same amount of space.

What fraction of the whole field does one game zone take up?

Problem Solving and Reasoning

7 Use these digit cards to make a fraction multiplication with the smallest possible answer.

 `1` `2` `5` `8`

Can you think of a rule that will always give you the smallest answer for any digits?

 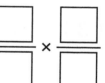

8 The square below has been split into thirds, then each third divided into smaller sections. What fraction of the large square is shaded?

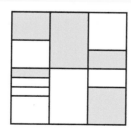

Did you know which calculations to do?

Fractions of Amounts

1 Work out:

$\frac{1}{9}$ of 27 = ☐ $\frac{1}{6}$ of 42 = ☐ $\frac{1}{15}$ of 60 = ☐

2 Find the fractions of the amounts given. Use the bar models to help you.

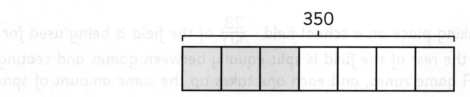

350

$\frac{1}{7}$ of 350 = ☐ $\frac{3}{7}$ of 350 = ☐ $\frac{4}{7}$ of 350 = ☐

360

$\frac{1}{12}$ of 360 = ☐ $\frac{5}{12}$ of 360 = ☐ $\frac{7}{12}$ of 360 = ☐

3 Find the fractions of these measures.

$\frac{4}{5}$ of 200 m = ☐ m $\frac{11}{20}$ of 400 ml = ☐ ml

$\frac{5}{8}$ of 480 g = ☐ g $\frac{7}{18}$ of 180 cm = ☐ cm

4 Nicole has read $\frac{4}{11}$ of a 264-page book. How many pages has she read?

5 Kenzo has drunk $\frac{3}{25}$ of a 1-litre bottle of water.
How many millilitres of water has he drunk?

☐ ml

6 Nina has run $\frac{7}{30}$ of a 1500 m race.
How much further does she have left to run?

☐ m

7 Milo has knitted $\frac{7}{9}$ of a 1.35 m long scarf.
How many more cm of the scarf does he need to knit?

Did you use the
same method as
your partner?

☐ cm

Problem Solving and Reasoning

8 Work out the numbers that make these calculations correct.

$$\frac{\square}{8} \text{ of } 640 = 560$$

$$\frac{5}{\square} \text{ of } 240 = 200$$

$$\frac{\square}{5} \text{ of } 30 = 48$$

9 Tabitha and Paulo each choose a number from the box.

45	60	48
49	50	75

Paulo says, "Two-thirds of my number is the
same as three-fifths of Tabitha's number."
Which number did each child choose?

Tabitha: ☐   Paulo: ☐

Can you find fractions of amounts?   ☑   ☑   ☑

Fractions of Amounts (Finding the Whole)

1 Using the bar models to help you, find the whole amount from the fraction given.

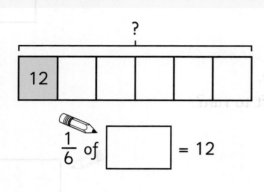

$\frac{1}{6}$ of ☐ = 12

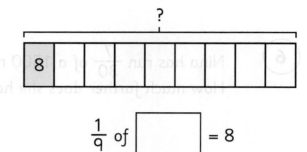

$\frac{1}{9}$ of ☐ = 8

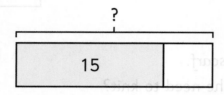

$\frac{3}{4}$ of ☐ = 15

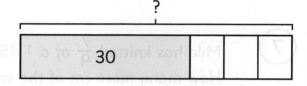

$\frac{5}{8}$ of ☐ = 30

2 Find the whole amount from the fraction given.

$\frac{1}{12}$ of ☐ = 8 $\frac{6}{7}$ of ☐ = 54 $\frac{4}{9}$ of ☐ = 24

3 Luna has eaten 10 grapes, which is $\frac{2}{15}$ of a bunch. How many grapes were in the whole bunch?

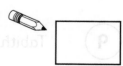

4 Danny describes $\frac{3}{20}$ of his rock collection as 'shiny'. He has 12 'shiny' rocks. How many rocks are in his collection?

5 Diego uses 100 ml of milk on his cereal. Nancy uses 250 ml of milk to make a milkshake. Between them, they have used $\frac{7}{10}$ of a bottle of milk.

How much milk was there in the full bottle?

| ml |

6 Juliet is $\frac{8}{25}$ of the way into a long journey. She has travelled 64 miles so far. How far does she have left to travel?

| miles |

7 $\frac{8}{13}$ of the people on a coach are children and the rest are adults. There are 15 adults on the coach.

How many people are there on the coach in total?

| |

Problem Solving and Reasoning

8 Uzman has come up with a rule for finding a whole amount:

> To find the whole from the fraction, you divide by the numerator and multiply by the denominator.

Do you agree with Uzman? Explain your reasoning.

| |

Are you able to find the whole?

Metric Units

1   Fill in the missing gaps in these sentences.

The mass of a banana is best measured in [ ].

My new kitchen sink has a [ ] of 20 litres.

There are [ ] kilograms in one tonne.

> How is the banana's weight different to its mass?

2   Choose the most sensible estimate for each of these measurements from the box.

15 cm   200 g
3 litres
20 g
1.5 m
15 m
2 kg   30 ml
300 ml   15 mm

The mass of this book. [ ]

The length of a pencil. [ ]

The capacity of a mug. [ ]

Problem Solving and Reasoning

3   Tim the stuntman is measuring the mass of his stunt truck.

Circle the **least appropriate** unit of measurement for Tim to use.

   Grams   Kilograms   Tonnes

Explain your reasoning.

[ ]

How did you measure up?   😕 ✓   😐 ✓   😊 ✓

Converting Metric Units

1 Complete these sentences. The first one has been done for you.

To convert from centimetres to millimetres you <u>multiply by 10</u>.

To convert from kilograms to grams you [ ].

To convert from millilitres to litres you [ ].

2 Circle the bigger amount in each pair of measurements.

$5\frac{1}{4}$ kg   500 g   20 m   800 cm

0.72 kg   900 g   1.5 km   2000 m

3 Complete these capacity conversions.

7 litres = [ ] ml   2500 ml = [ ] litres

$8\frac{1}{2}$ litres = [ ] ml   6712 ml = [ ] litres

4 The mass of a rucksack is shown on the scale.

What is the mass of the rucksack in grams?

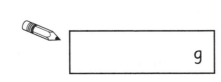

[ ] g

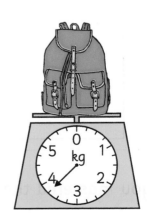

Block 5 — Converting Units — Step 2

5 A carton of juice contains 220 ml and a bottle of juice contains 2.1 litres.

Is there more juice in ten cartons or one bottle? Circle the correct answer.

| Ten cartons | | One bottle |

6 The lengths of three ribbons are shown in the table.

Ribbon A	Ribbon B	Ribbon C
159 mm	17 cm	0.019 m

Which ribbon is the longest?

Problem Solving and Reasoning

7 Mira is converting units of capacity.

When converting from litres to millilitres, the number of millilitres will always end in a 0.

Do you agree with Mira?
Explain your answer.

8 What should you multiply by to convert from millimetres to kilometres? Explain your reasoning.

Have you mastered the metric units?

Calculations with Metric Units

1 Work out the missing measurements on these bar models.

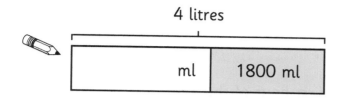

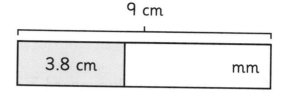

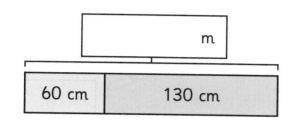

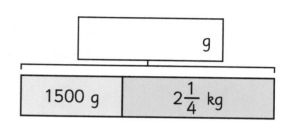

2 Complete these measurement calculations.

$1\frac{1}{2}$ litres + 800 ml = ⬚ ml   2.7 kg + 250 g = ⬚ g

1.9 m + 50 cm = ⬚ m   7.54 km + 300 m = ⬚ km

3 A bottle of ketchup contains 300 ml.

How many litres of ketchup are in 5 bottles?

 litres

4 How many 10 cm crayons would you have to put end to end to make a line of crayons that is $8\frac{1}{5}$ m long?

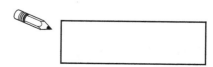

5 There are 200 g of strawberries in a small tub
and 800 g of strawberries in a large tub.

What is the mass of strawberries in 7 small tubs
and 3 large tubs? Give your answer in kilograms.

[ ] kg

6 Stevie the slug moved 5.3 cm in the first hour of the day,
88 mm in the second hour and 0.18 m in the third hour.

How many millimetres further did Stevie
move in the second hour than the first?

[ ] mm

How many centimetres did Stevie move in total in the three hours?

[ ] cm

Problem Solving and Reasoning

7 Gabe has some carrots, potatoes and onions.
The carrots have a mass of $2\frac{1}{2}$ kg.
The potatoes have half the mass of the carrots.
The onions are 855 g heavier than the potatoes.

What is the mass of the onions in kilograms?

> Is it easier to work in
> grams or kilograms?
> Discuss with your partner.

[ ] kg

What is the total mass, in grams, of the carrots, potatoes and onions?

[ ] g

How well can you calculate with units? 😕 ✓ 🙂 ✓ 😉 ✓

Kilometres and Miles

1 5 miles ≈ 8 kilometres

1 mile		1 mile		1 mile		1 mile		1 mile	
1 km	1 km	1 km	1 km	1 km	1 km	1 km	1 km

Use this fact to complete the approximate conversion tables below.

Miles	Kilometres
5	
20	
50	

Miles	Kilometres
	16
	48
	800

2 A car tyre should be replaced after 32 000 km.

Approximately how many miles is this?

km

3 Jane walked 60 miles in June and 100 km in July.

Approximately how many kilometres further did she walk in July than in June?

km

Problem Solving and Reasoning

4 Lucy is trying to cycle 15 miles. Her fitness tracker says she has cycled 24 km, but that she still has further to go.

Why do you think this might be?

FURTHER!

Do you know your miles from your smiles?

Imperial Units

1 Complete this scale to show the conversions between pounds and ounces.

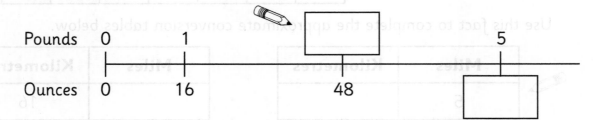

Pounds	0	1			5
Ounces	0	16	48		

2 Use the facts that 1 foot = 12 inches and 1 inch ≈ 2.5 cm
to convert these measurements and complete the calculations.

60 inches = ☐ feet

$4\frac{1}{2}$ feet + 4 inches = ☐ inches

30 inches ≈ ☐ cm

20 inches − 13 cm ≈ ☐ cm

3 A cow produces $2\frac{1}{2}$ gallons of milk every day.

How many pints of milk will the cow produce in a week?
1 gallon = 8 pints

Is it easier to use imperial
or metric units? Why?

☐ pints

Problem Solving and Reasoning

4 Arlo says, "The number of pints in 50 gallons is
greater than the number of ounces in 2 stone."

Do you agree with Arlo? Explain your answer.

8 pints = 1 gallon
1 stone = 14 pounds
1 pound = 16 ounces

Have you conquered the imperial units?